To Celebrate

_____

_____

Date

_____

THANK YOU FOR COMING.

Let's celebrate!

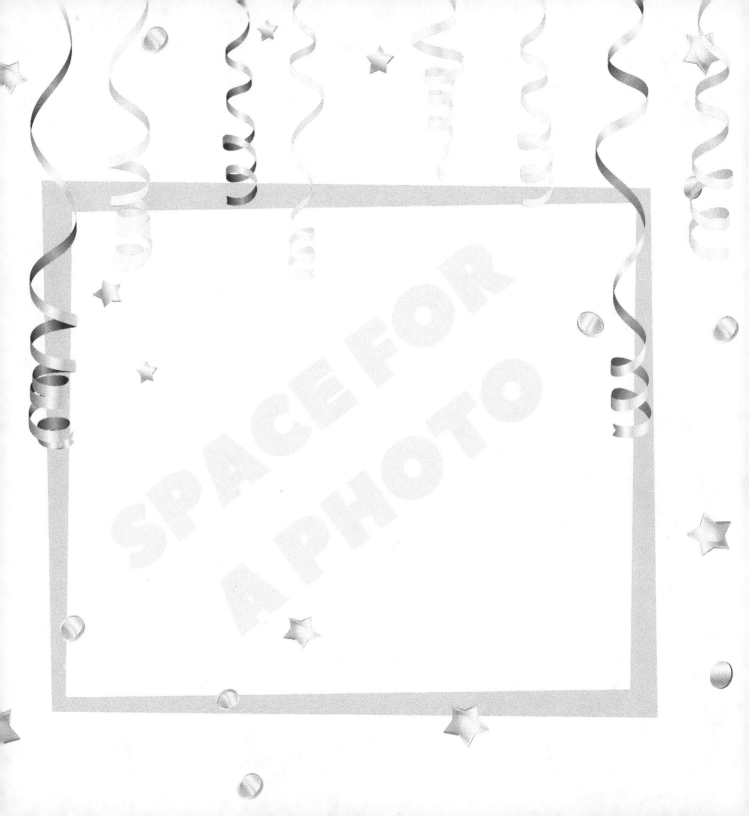

Guest Name

_____

Wishes & Messages

_____

_____

_____

_____

_____

_____

EMAIL/PHONE

Guest Name

Wishes & Messages

Email/Phone

Guest Name

_____

Wishes & Messages

_____

_____

_____

_____

_____

_____

EMAIL/PHONE

Guest Name

_____

Wishes & Messages

_____

_____

_____

_____

_____

EMAIL/PHONE
_____

Guest Name

_____

Wishes & Messages

_____

_____

_____

_____

_____

_____

Email/Phone

Guest Name

_____

Wishes & Messages

_____

_____

_____

_____

_____

_____

EMAIL/PHONE

Guest Name

_____

Wishes & Messages

_____

_____

_____

_____

_____

_____

Email/Phone

Guest Name

_____

Wishes & Messages

_____

_____

_____

_____

_____

_____

EMAIL/PHONE

Guest Name

_____

Wishes & Messages

_____

_____

_____

_____

_____

_____

EMAIL/PHONE _____

Guest Name

_____

Wishes & Messages

_____

_____

_____

_____

_____

_____

Email/Phone _____

Guest Name

_____

Wishes & Messages

_____

_____

_____

_____

_____

_____

EMAIL/PHONE _____

Guest Name

_____

Wishes & Messages

_____

_____

_____

_____

_____

_____

EMAIL/PHONE

Guest Name

_____

Wishes & Messages

_____

_____

_____

_____

_____

_____

EMAIL/PHONE

Guest Name

Wishes & Messages

EMAIL/PHONE

Guest Name

_____

Wishes & Messages

_____

_____

_____

_____

_____

_____

EMAIL/PHONE
_____

Guest Name

_____

Wishes & Messages

_____

_____

_____

_____

_____

EMAIL/PHONE _____

Guest Name

_____

Wishes & Messages

_____

_____

_____

_____

_____

_____

EMAIL/PHONE _____

Guest Name

_____

Wishes & Messages

_____

_____

_____

_____

_____

Email/Phone _____

Guest Name

_____

Wishes & Messages

_____

_____

_____

_____

_____

_____

EMAIL/PHONE
_____

Guest Name

_____

Wishes & Messages

_____

_____

_____

_____

_____

_____

EMAIL/PHONE
_____

Guest Name

_____

Wishes & Messages

_____

_____

_____

_____

_____

_____

EMAIL/PHONE

Guest Name

_____

Wishes & Messages

_____

_____

_____

_____

_____

_____

EMAIL/PHONE

Guest Name

_____

Wishes & Messages

_____

_____

_____

_____

_____

_____

EMAIL/PHONE
_____

Guest Name

Wishes & Messages

EMAIL/PHONE

Guest Name

_____

Wishes & Messages

_____

_____

_____

_____

_____

_____

EMAIL/PHONE

Guest Name

_____

Wishes & Messages

_____

_____

_____

_____

_____

Email/Phone _____

Guest Name

_____

Wishes & Messages

_____

_____

_____

_____

_____

_____

EMAIL/PHONE

Guest Name

Wishes & Messages

Email/Phone

Guest Name

Wishes & Messages

EMAIL/PHONE

Guest Name

_____

Wishes & Messages

_____

_____

_____

_____

_____

EMAIL/PHONE _____

Guest Name

_____

Wishes & Messages

_____

_____

_____

_____

_____

EMAIL/PHONE

Guest Name

Wishes & Messages

EMAIL/PHONE

Guest Name

_____

Wishes & Messages

_____

_____

_____

_____

_____

_____

EMAIL/PHONE

Guest Name

_____

Wishes & Messages

_____

_____

_____

_____

_____

Email/Phone
_____

Guest Name

_____

Wishes & Messages

_____

_____

_____

_____

_____

_____

_____

EMAIL/PHONE

Guest Name

_____

Wishes & Messages

_____

_____

_____

_____

_____

Email/Phone _____

Guest Name

Wishes & Messages

EMAIL/PHONE

Guest Name

Wishes & Messages

Email/Phone

Guest Name

_____

Wishes & Messages

_____

_____

_____

_____

_____

_____

EMAIL/PHONE
_____

Guest Name

_____

Wishes & Messages

_____

_____

_____

_____

_____

_____
Email/Phone

Guest Name

_____

Wishes & Messages

_____

_____

_____

_____

_____

_____

EMAIL/PHONE

Guest Name

_____

Wishes & Messages

_____

_____

_____

_____

_____

EMAIL/PHONE
_____

Guest Name

Wishes & Messages

EMAIL/PHONE

Guest Name

Wishes & Messages

_____

_____

_____

_____

_____

_____

EMAIL/PHONE _____

Guest Name

_____

Wishes & Messages

_____

_____

_____

_____

_____

EMAIL/PHONE

Guest Name

Wishes & Messages

Email/Phone

Guest Name

_____

Wishes & Messages

_____

_____

_____

_____

_____

_____

Email/Phone

Guest Name

_____

Wishes & Messages

_____

_____

_____

_____

_____

EMAIL/PHONE _____

Guest Name

_____

Wishes & Messages

_____

_____

_____

_____

_____

_____

Email/Phone
_____

Guest Name

_____

Wishes & Messages

_____

_____

_____

_____

_____

Email/Phone
_____

Guest Name

_____

Wishes & Messages

_____

_____

_____

_____

_____

_____

EMAIL/PHONE
_____

Guest Name

_____

Wishes & Messages

_____

_____

_____

_____

_____

EMAIL/PHONE _____

Guest Name
_____

Wishes & Messages

_____
_____
_____
_____
_____
_____

EMAIL/PHONE
_____

Guest Name

_____

Wishes & Messages

_____

_____

_____

_____

_____

EMAIL/PHONE
_____

Guest Name

_____

Wishes & Messages

_____

_____

_____

_____

_____

_____

EMAIL/PHONE
_____

Guest Name

_____

Wishes & Messages

_____

_____

_____

_____

_____

EMAIL/PHONE
_____

Guest Name

_____

Wishes & Messages

_____

_____

_____

_____

_____

_____

EMAIL/PHONE _____

Guest Name

_____

Wishes & Messages

_____

_____

_____

_____

_____

_____

Email/Phone

Guest Name

_____

Wishes & Messages

_____

_____

_____

_____

_____

_____

EMAIL/PHONE _____

Guest Name

Wishes & Messages

EMAIL/PHONE

Guest Name

_____

Wishes & Messages

_____

_____

_____

_____

_____

_____

EMAIL/PHONE

Guest Name

_____

Wishes & Messages

_____

_____

_____

_____

_____

EMAIL/PHONE
_____

Guest Name

_____

Wishes & Messages

_____

_____

_____

_____

_____

_____

EMAIL/PHONE
_____

Guest Name

Wishes & Messages

EMAIL/PHONE

Guest Name

_____

Wishes & Messages

_____

_____

_____

_____

_____

_____

EMAIL/PHONE _____

Guest Name

Wishes & Messages

Email/Phone

Guest Name

Wishes & Messages

EMAIL/PHONE

Guest Name

_____

Wishes & Messages

_____

_____

_____

_____

_____

_____

Email/Phone
_____

Guest Name

_____

Wishes & Messages

_____

_____

_____

_____

_____

EMAIL/PHONE
_____

Guest Name

_____

Wishes & Messages

_____

_____

_____

_____

_____

_____

Email/Phone _____

Guest Name

_____

Wishes & Messages

_____

_____

_____

_____

_____

_____

EMAIL/PHONE
_____

Guest Name

Wishes & Messages

EMAIL/PHONE

Guest Name

_____

Wishes & Messages

_____

_____

_____

_____

_____

_____

EMAIL/PHONE

Guest Name

_____

Wishes & Messages

_____

_____

_____

_____

_____

_____

Email/Phone

Guest Name

_____

Wishes & Messages

_____

_____

_____

_____

_____

_____

Email/Phone
_____

Guest Name

Wishes & Messages

EMAIL/PHONE

Guest Name

_____

Wishes & Messages

_____

_____

_____

_____

_____

_____

EMAIL/PHONE

Guest Name

_____

Wishes & Messages

_____

_____

_____

_____

_____

_____

Email/Phone

Guest Name

_____

Wishes & Messages

_____

_____

_____

_____

_____

_____

Email/Phone
_____

Guest Name

_____

Wishes & Messages

_____

_____

_____

_____

_____

EMAIL/PHONE _____

Guest Name

_____

Wishes & Messages

_____

_____

_____

_____

_____

_____

EMAIL/PHONE

Guest Name

Wishes & Messages

EMAIL/PHONE

Guest Name

_____

Wishes & Messages

_____

_____

_____

_____

_____

_____

EMAIL/PHONE _____

Guest Name

_____

Wishes & Messages

_____

_____

_____

_____

_____

_____

EMAIL/PHONE _____

Guest Name

_____

Wishes & Messages

_____

_____

_____

_____

_____

_____

EMAIL/PHONE

Guest Name

Wishes & Messages

Email/Phone

Guest Name

_____

Wishes & Messages

_____

_____

_____

_____

_____

_____

EMAIL/PHONE

Guest Name

_____

Wishes & Messages

_____

_____

_____

_____

_____

EMAIL/PHONE _____

Guest Name

Wishes & Messages

EMAIL/PHONE

Guest Name

Wishes & Messages

Email/Phone

Guest Name

Wishes & Messages

Email/Phone

Guest Name

_____

Wishes & Messages

_____

_____

_____

_____

_____

EMAIL/PHONE
_____

Guest Name

_____

Wishes & Messages

_____

_____

_____

_____

_____

_____

EMAIL/PHONE
_____

Guest Name

_____

Wishes & Messages

_____

_____

_____

_____

_____

_____

Email/Phone

Guest Name

_____

Wishes & Messages

_____

_____

_____

_____

_____

_____

EMAIL/PHONE

Guest Name

Wishes & Messages

EMAIL/PHONE

Guest Name

_____

Wishes & Messages

_____

_____

_____

_____

_____

_____

EMAIL/PHONE

Guest Name

_____

Wishes & Messages

_____

_____

_____

_____

_____

_____

Email/Phone _____

Guest Name

_____

Wishes & Messages

_____

_____

_____

_____

_____

_____

EMAIL/PHONE
_____

Guest Name

_____

Wishes & Messages

_____

_____

_____

_____

_____

EMAIL/PHONE _____

Guest Name

_____

Wishes & Messages

_____

_____

_____

_____

_____

_____

EMAIL/PHONE
_____

Guest Name

_____

Wishes & Messages

_____

_____

_____

_____

_____

_____

EMAIL/PHONE _____

Guest Name

Wishes & Messages

Email/Phone

Guest Name

_____

Wishes & Messages

_____

_____

_____

_____

_____

_____

EMAIL/PHONE
_____

Guest Name

_____

Wishes & Messages

_____

_____

_____

_____

_____

_____

EMAIL/PHONE

NOTES & PHOTOS

NOTES & PHOTOS

NOTES & PHOTOS

NOTES & PHOTOS

NOTES & PHOTOS

GIFT LOG

Name / Email / Phone	Gift

GIFT LOG

Name / Email / Phone	Gift

GIFT LOG

Name / Email / Phone	Gift

GIFT LOG

Name / Email / Phone	Gift

GIFT LOG

Name / Email / Phone	Gift

GIFT LOG

Name / Email / Phone	Gift

GIFT LOG

Name / Email / Phone	Gift

Printed in the USA
CPSIA information can be obtained
at www.ICGtesting.com
LVHW070327210124
769296LV00007B/63

9 788395 823428